A PICTURE BOOK OF
Dolley and James Madison

by David A. Adler and Michael S. Adler
illustrated by Ronald Himler

Holiday House / New York

Text copyright © 2009 by David A. Adler and Michael S. Adler
Illustrations copyright © 2009 by Ronald Himler
All Rights Reserved
Printed and Bound in Malaysia
www.holidayhouse.com
First Edition
1 3 5 7 9 10 8 6 4 2

Library of Congress Cataloging-in-Publication Data
Adler, David A.
A picture book of Dolley and James Madison / by David A. Adler and Michael S. Adler ;
illustrated by Ronald Himler. — 1st ed.
p. cm.
ISBN-13: 978-0-8234-2009-4 (hardcover)
1. Madison, James, 1751–1836—Juvenile literature. 2. Madison, Dolley, 1768–1849—Juvenile literature.
3. Presidents—United States—Biography—Juvenile literature. 4. Presidents' spouses—United States—
Biography—Juvenile literature. I. Adler, Michael S. II. Himler, Ronald., ill. III. Title.
E342.A64 2009
973.51092—dc22
[B]
2007041178

To My Parents
—M. S. A.

Washington, D.C., was burning, set afire by enemy British troops. President James Madison was with American soldiers in nearby Maryland. His wife, Dolley, was in the Executive Mansion, now called the White House.

"Will you believe it," she wrote to her sister. "I am still here within sound of cannon! Mr. Madison comes not; May God protect him."

The War of 1812 was not going well for the Americans. Mrs. Madison was told to run for her life; but first she took several paintings and put them in her carriage. She wanted to save a large portrait of President Washington, but it was screwed to the wall. Dolley Madison cut it from its frame, rolled it up, and took it with her as she hurried off. The Executive Mansion burned that night, but President James and Dolley Madison and some of the young nation's greatest treasures were safe.

James Madison, America's fourth president, was born in Port Conway, Virginia, on March 16, 1751. He was the first of twelve children born to James and Nelly Madison. His father, James, was a justice of the peace, the commander of the local militia, and the owner of a large plantation and many slaves. His wife, Nelly, was a small, frail-looking woman who managed to raise a large family and live to age ninety-eight.

Young James Madison was taught by his paternal grandmother to read, write, and do simple arithmetic. Then, in 1762, he was sent seventy miles away to a boarding school. In 1769 he entered the College of New Jersey, now Princeton University.

Madison was short but lively. People liked him. At first he thought of becoming a preacher or lawyer, but he was drawn to politics.

It was a time of interesting politics. At the start of the 1770s most of the people in the thirteen American colonies were loyal to the king of England. But taxes and the many British soldiers in the colonies led to unrest and the Revolution. By the end of the decade, a new nation, the United States of America, had been formed.

In 1776 Madison was elected to the Virginia Convention, which voted for independence from England. There he played a key role in drafting Virginia's new constitution.

In 1780 Madison was a delegate to the Second Continental Congress. He and others argued for a stronger central government. By 1787 it was clear that they were right, and a Constitutional Convention was called.

Madison drafted the Virginia Plan. It called for three branches of government, with the legislative branch divided in two. The number of each state's delegates would be based on its population. This favored states with many citizens. Representatives of small states would not agree to such a plan. They wanted all states to have an equal number of delegates, so the "Great Compromise" was reached. Seats in the House of Representatives were set according to population. In the Senate states received equal representation.

Many states hesitated to ratify the Constitution without some guarantees of people's rights, so Madison drafted the Bill of Rights. It guarantees for all Americans the freedom of speech, press, and religion.

For his work, Madison earned the nickname the Father of the Constitution.

Madison was elected to the first Congress, where he served as a member of the House of Representatives until 1797. It was during this time that he began to court Dorothea "Dolley" Payne Todd.

Dolley was born May 20, 1768, on a farm in New Garden, North Carolina. She was the third of nine children born to John Payne Jr. and Mary Coles Payne. Future president James Monroe later described her as a tomboy. She often had foot races with Monroe, and sometimes won.

In 1783 the Paynes sold their tobacco plantation, freed their slaves, and moved to Philadelphia. There Dolley went to a Quaker school.

During the Constitutional Convention many delegates visited the Paynes in their large Philadelphia house, and Dolley charmed them. Benjamin Franklin told her she was "the most beautiful young lady in America." James Madison visited, too, but didn't seem taken with the pretty, but much younger, Dolley Payne. And she did not take any real notice of the short, balding James Madison.

Among the many men interested in Dolley was John Todd, a successful young lawyer. They courted, and on January 7, 1790, they married. They had two sons, John and William.

William was born in July 1793, in the midst of a yellow fever epidemic. First John Todd's parents were stricken and died. Then he and baby William died of the disease.

While Dolley mourned, many people came to visit, including Martha Washington, Thomas Jefferson, and James Madison. After the mourning period ended, Madison kept visiting.

James and Dolley went riding together. He brought gifts for her young son, John. On September 15, 1794, James and Dolley married. They remained in Philadelphia until 1797, when Madison left Congress and Dolley and John returned to Madison's home in Virginia.

In 1800 Madison's friend and fellow Virginian Thomas Jefferson was elected president. He made Madison his secretary of state. During Madison's time as secretary, the United States purchased the Louisiana Territory from France. On the seas, thousands of American sailors were captured and forced to join the British navy. The French also seized American ships. Madison helped get the Embargo Act passed, which cut off trade with both countries.

Dolley also played a key role in the Jefferson administration, serving as the widowed president's official hostess. Senator John Quincy Adams attended some of the many dinner parties she organized and described her as beautiful, lively, charming, and a sensible hostess.

After two terms as president, Jefferson supported
Madison to succeed him. Madison made no campaign
speeches. Still, he easily won over Charles Pinckney of
South Carolina. He was president for two terms, from
1809 until 1817.

It was a difficult time to be president. The French and British were at war. Warships from both nations, but especially Great Britain, were seizing American ships. The Embargo Act aimed at ending the problem hurt American trade more than it hurt the French and British. On June 18, 1812, Madison and his secretary of state, James Monroe, with the approval of Congress, declared war on Great Britain.

At first the war did not go well for the United States. There were early defeats at Buffalo, Detroit, and elsewhere. In April 1813 American soldiers sailed across Lake Ontario and set fire to two Parliament buildings in Canada. In August 1814 the British struck back and burned much of Washington, D.C.

In December 1814 the Americans and the British signed a peace treaty. The treaty didn't address the issues that started the war, but at least it ended it.

Throughout Madison's two terms as president, Dolley held "Wednesday drawing rooms," afternoon parties at which she served cakes, cookies, ice cream, and fruit to her guests. Also, with money from Congress, she redecorated the Executive Mansion.

At the end of his second term, Madison helped his close friend James Monroe secure the presidency. Then he and Dolley retired to Virginia.

Madison helped found the University of Virginia and organized his many papers, including those from the Constitutional Convention.

James Madison died on June 28, 1836, at the age of eighty-five. Many years later, President John F. Kennedy described Madison as "our most underrated President."

After her husband's death, Dolley Madison returned to Washington, D.C. She was a respected hostess and welcome guest of Congressmen and presidents. Senator Henry Clay once said, "Everybody loves Mrs. Madison." To many of her admirers she was "Queen Dolley."

Dolley Madison died on July 12, 1849, at the age of eighty-one. President Zachary Taylor declared the day of her funeral a time of national mourning.

James and Dolley Madison are buried side by side at their home in Montpelier, Virginia.

IMPORTANT DATES

1751   James Madison born in Port Conway, Virginia, March 16.

1768   Dolley Payne born on a farm in New Garden, North Carolina, May 20.

1769   James enrolls at the College of New Jersey.

1773   James elected to Committee of Safety.

1776   James serves as a delegate to the Virginia Convention.

1787   Constitutional Convention convenes in Philadelphia.

1790   Dolley and John Todd wed, January 7.

1794   James and Dolley marry, September 15.

1801   James appointed secretary of state. Dolley becomes official hostess.

1808   James elected president.

1812   Congress declares war against Great Britain, June.

1814   British troops burn Washington, D.C., August 24.

1817   Madisons retire to Montpelier, Virginia.

1836   James dies, June 28.

1849   Dolley dies, July 12.

AUTHORS' NOTES

There are many who write *Dolly*, instead of *Dolley*, including Lucia B. Cutts, her grandniece and biographer. But in her will, it's spelled *Dolley*, so it was likely Mrs. Madison's favored spelling.

According to Noel B. Gerson, author of *The Velvet Glove: A Life of Dolly Madison*, in 1787 thirty-six-year-old James Madison visited the Payne family; but he was not impressed by nineteen-year-old Dolley.

On the issue of slavery, Madison wrote in an 1825 letter, "The magnitude of this evil among us is so deeply felt, and so universally acknowledged, that no merit could be greater than devising a satisfactory remedy for it." Nonetheless, he had many slaves working on his plantation in Montpelier.

One possible reason the United States declared war on Great Britain in 1812 and not France, whose warships also seized American ships, was the hope of taking Canada and using it as a bargaining chip to settle all future grievances. The Americans believed Canada was poorly protected by the British and would be easy to conquer.

SOURCE NOTES

Each source note includes the first word or words and the last word or words of a quotation and its source. References are to books cited in the Selected Bibliography.

"Will you . . . protect him.": Peterson, p. 346.
"the most . . . in America.": Gerson, p. 44.
"our most . . . President.": Padover, p. 252.
"Everybody . . . Madison.": Allgor, p. 232.

SELECTED BIBLIOGRAPHY

Allgor, Catherine. *A Perfect Union: Dolley Madison and the Creation of the American Nation*. New York: Henry Holt, 2006.

Gay, Sydney Howard. *James Madison*. Boston: Houghton, Mifflin, 1899.

Gerson, Noel B. *The Velvet Glove: A Life of Dolly Madison*. Nashville, TN: Thomas Nelson Inc., 1975.

Moore, Virginia. *The Madisons: A Biography*. New York: McGraw-Hill Education, 1979.

Padover, Saul K. *The Complete Madison*. New York: Harper, 1953.

Peterson, Merrill D., ed. *James Madison, A Biography in His Own Words*, Vols. 1 and 2. New York: Newsweek, 1974.

Rutland, Robert Allen. *James Madison: The Founding Father*. New York: Macmillan, 1987.

Schumach, Murray. "She Spelled It Dolley Madison." *New York Times*, April 13, 1958, p. 1.

Wills, Garry. *James Madison*. New York: Time Books, 2002.

RECOMMENDED WEBSITES

www.whitehouse.gov/history/presidents/jm4.html

www.virginia.edu/pjm/

www.jamesmadisonmus.org